God loves you just the way you are,

but he refuses to leave you that way.

He wants you to have . . .

A Heart
Like Jesus

Max Lucado

W PUBLISHING GROUP™

www.wpublishinggroup.com

A Division of Thomas Nelson, Inc.
www.ThomasNelson.com

Published by W Publishing Group, a division of Thomas Nelson, Inc., P. O. Box 141000, Nashville, Tenneessee 37214.

Compiled by Nancy Guthrie.

Unless otherwise indicated, Scripture quotations used in this book are from the Holy Bible, New Century Version, copyright © 1987, 1988, 1991 by Word Publishing, Nashville, Tennessee 37214. Used by permission.

Other Scripture references are from the following sources:
The Holy Bible, New International Version (NIV), copyright © 1973, 1978, 1984, International Bible Society. Used by permission of Zondervan Bible Publishers. The King James Version of the Bible (KJV). The Living Bible (TLB), copyright © 1971 by Tyndale House Publishers, Wheaton, Ill. Used by permission. The Message (MSG), copyright © 1993. Used by permission of NavPress Publishing Group. J. B. Phillips: The New Testament in Modern English, Revised Edition (PHILLIPS), copyright © J. B. Phillips 1958, 1960, 1972. Used by permission of Macmillan Publishing Co., Inc. New American Standard Bible (NASB), © 1960, 1977 by the Lockman Foundation. The Revised Standard Version of the Bible (RSV), copyright © 1946, 1952, 1971, 1973 by the Division of Christian Education of the National Council of the Churches of Christ in the USA. Used by permission.

Excerpted from Max Lucado, *Just Like Jesus* (Nashville: W Publishing Group, 1998).

Library of Congress Cataloging-in-Publication Data

Lucado, Max.
   A heart like Jesus / by Max Lucado.
      p. cm.
Includes bibliographical references.
   ISBN 0-8499-1774-3 (hardcover)
   1. Christian life. I. Title.
BV4501.3 L84 2003
248.4—dc21   2002015332

Printed in the United States of America
02 03 04 05 06 07 PHX 9 8 7 6 5 4 3 2 1

To Dennis and Patty McDonald . . .
thanking God for your mighty prayers
and tender touches.

OTHER BOOKS BY MAX LUCADO

Contents

CONTENTS

Chapter One

A Heart Like Jesus

WHAT IF, FOR ONE DAY, JESUS WERE TO become you? What if, for twenty-four hours, Jesus wakes up in your bed, walks in your shoes, lives in your house, assumes your schedule? Your boss becomes his boss, your mother becomes his mother, your pains become his pains? With one exception, nothing about your life changes. Your health doesn't change. Your circumstances don't change. Your schedule isn't altered. Your problems aren't solved. Only one change occurs.

What if, for one day and one night, Jesus lives your life with his heart? Your heart gets the day off, and your life is led by the heart of Christ. His priorities govern your actions. His passions drive your decisions. His love directs your behavior.

What would you be like? Would people notice a change? Your family—would they see something new? Your coworkers—would they sense a difference? What about the less fortunate? Would you treat them the same? And your friends? Would they detect more joy? How about your enemies? Would they receive more mercy from Christ's heart than from yours?

And you? How would you feel? What alterations would this transplant have on your stress level? Your mood swings? Your temper? Would you sleep better? Would you see sunsets differently? Death differently? Taxes differently? Any chance you'd need fewer aspirin or sedatives? How about your reaction to traffic delays? (Ouch, that touched a nerve.) Would you still dread what you are dreading? Better yet, would you still do what you are doing?

Would you still do what you had planned to do for the next twenty-four hours? Pause and think about your schedule. Obligations. Engagements. Outings. Appointments. With Jesus taking over your heart, would anything change?

Keep working on this for a moment. Adjust the lens of your imagination until you have a clear picture of Jesus leading your life, then snap the shutter and frame the image. What you see is what God wants. He wants you to "think and act like Christ Jesus" (Phil. 2:5).

God's plan for you is nothing short of a new heart. If you were a car, God would want control of your engine. If you were a computer, God would claim the software and the hard drive. If you were an airplane, he'd take his seat in the cockpit. But you are a person, so God wants to change your heart.

"But you were taught to be made new in your hearts, to become a new person. That new person is made to be like God—made to be truly good and holy" (Eph. 4:23–24).

God wants you to be just like Jesus. He wants you to have a heart like his.

I'm going to risk something here. It's dangerous to sum up grand truths in one statement, but I'm going to try. If a sentence or two could capture God's desire for each of us, it might read like this:

God loves you just the way you are, but he refuses to leave you that way. He wants you to be just like Jesus.

God loves you just the way you are. If you think his love for you would be stronger if your faith were, you are wrong. If you think his love would be deeper if your thoughts were, wrong again. Don't confuse God's love with the love of people. The love of people often increases with performance and decreases with mistakes. Not so with God's love. He loves you right where you are. To quote my wife's favorite author:

God's love never ceases. Never. Though we spurn him. Ignore him. Reject him. Despise him. Disobey

4

him. He will not change. Our evil cannot diminish his love. Our goodness cannot increase it. Our faith does not earn it anymore than our stupidity jeopardizes it. God doesn't love us less if we fail or more if we succeed. God's love never ceases.[1]

God loves you just the way you are, but he refuses to leave you that way.

Where did we get the idea we can't change? From whence come statements such as, "It's just my nature to worry," or, "I'll always be pessimistic. I'm just that way," or, "I have a bad temper. I can't help the way I react"? Who says? Would we make similar statements about our bodies? "It's just my nature to have a broken leg. I can't do anything about it." Of course not. If our bodies malfunction, we seek help. Shouldn't we do the same with our hearts? Shouldn't we seek aid for our sour attitudes? Can't we request treatment for our selfish tirades? Of course we can. Jesus can change our hearts. He wants us to have a heart like his.

Can you imagine a better offer?

The Heart of Christ

The heart of Jesus was pure. The Savior was adored by thousands, yet content to live a simple life. He was cared for by women (Luke 8:1–3), yet never accused of lustful thoughts; scorned by his own creation, but willing to forgive them before they even requested his mercy. Peter, who traveled with Jesus for three and a half years, described him as a "lamb, unblemished and spotless" (1 Pet. 1:19 NASB). After spending the same amount of time with Jesus, John concluded, "And in him is no sin" (1 John 3:5 NIV).

Jesus' heart was peaceful. The disciples fretted over the need to feed the thousands, but not Jesus. He thanked God for the problem. The disciples shouted for fear in the storm, but not Jesus. He slept through it. Peter drew his sword to fight the soldiers, but not Jesus. He lifted his hand to heal. His heart was at peace. When his disciples abandoned him, did he pout and go home? When Peter denied him, did Jesus lose his temper? When the soldiers spit in his face, did he breathe fire in theirs? Far from it. He was at peace. He forgave them. He refused to be guided by vengeance.

He also refused to be guided by anything other than his high call. His heart was purposeful. Most lives aim at nothing in particular and achieve it. Jesus aimed at one goal—to save humanity from its sin. He could summarize his life with one sentence: "The Son of man came to seek and to save the lost" (Luke 19:10 RSV). Jesus was so focused on his task that he knew when to say, "My time has not yet come" (John 2:4) and when to say, "It is finished" (John 19:30). But he was not so focused on his goal that he was unpleasant.

Quite the contrary. How pleasant were his thoughts! Children couldn't resist Jesus. He could find beauty in lilies, joy in worship, and possibilities in problems. He would spend days with multitudes of sick people and still feel sorry for them. He spent over three decades wading through the muck and mire of our sin, yet still saw enough beauty in us to die for our mistakes.

But the crowning attribute of Christ was this: his heart was spiritual. His thoughts reflected his intimate relationship with the Father. "I am in the Father and the Father is in me," he stated (John 14:11). His first recorded sermon begins with the words, "The Spirit of the Lord is upon Me" (Luke 4:18 NASB). He was "led by the Spirit" (Matt. 4:1 NIV) and "full of the Holy Spirit" (Luke 4:1 NIV). He returned from the desert "in the power of the Spirit" (Luke 4:14 NIV).

Jesus took his instructions from God. It was his habit to go to worship (Luke 4:16). It was his practice to memorize Scripture (Luke 4:4). Luke says Jesus "often slipped away to be alone so he could pray" (Luke 5:16). His times of prayer guided him. He once returned from prayer and announced it was time to move to another city (Mark 1:38). Another time of prayer resulted in the selection of the disciples (Luke 6:12–13). Jesus was led by an unseen hand. "The Son does whatever the Father does" (John 5:19). In the same chapter he stated, "I

can do nothing alone. I judge only the way I am told"
(John 5:30).

The heart of Jesus was spiritual.

The Heart of Humanity

Our hearts seem so far from his. He is pure; we are
greedy. He is peaceful; we are hassled. He is purposeful; we are distracted. He is pleasant; we are
cranky. He is spiritual; we are earthbound. The distance between our hearts and his seems so immense.
How could we ever hope to have the heart of Jesus?

Ready for a surprise? You already do. You already
have the heart of Christ. Why are you looking at me
that way? Would I kid you? If you are in Christ, you
already have the heart of Christ. One of the supreme
yet unrealized promises of God is simply this: if you
have given your life to Jesus, Jesus has given himself
to you. He has made your heart his home. It would
be hard to say it more succinctly than Paul does:
"Christ lives in me" (Gal. 2:20 MSG).

At the risk of repeating myself, let me repeat myself. If you have given your life to Jesus, Jesus has given himself to you. He has moved in and unpacked his bags and is ready to change you "into his likeness from one degree of glory to another" (2 Cor. 3:18 RSV). Paul explains it with these words: "Strange as it seems, we Christians actually do have within us a portion of the very thoughts and mind of Christ" (1 Cor. 2:16 TLB).

Strange is the word! If I have the mind of Jesus, why do I still think so much like me? If I have the heart of Christ, why do I still have the hang-ups of Max? If Jesus dwells within me, why do I still hate traffic jams?

Part of the answer is illustrated in a story about a lady who had a small house on the seashore of Ireland at the turn of the century. She was quite wealthy but also quite frugal. The people were surprised, then, when she decided to be among the first to have electricity in her home.

Several weeks after the installation, a meter reader

A HEART LIKE JESUS

appeared at her door. He asked if her electricity was working well, and she assured him it was. "I'm wondering if you can explain something to me," he said. "Your meter shows scarcely any usage. Are you using your power?"

"Certainly," she answered. "Each evening when the sun sets, I turn on my lights just long enough to light my candles; then I turn them off."[2]

She's tapped into the power but doesn't use it. Her house is connected but not altered. Don't we make the same mistake? We, too—with our souls saved but our hearts unchanged—are connected but not altered. Trusting Christ for salvation but resisting transformation. We occasionally flip the switch, but most of the time we settle for shadows.

What would happen if we left the light on? What would happen if we not only flipped the switch but lived in the light? What changes would occur if we set about the task of dwelling in the radiance of Christ?

No doubt about it: God has ambitious plans for us. The same one who saved your soul longs to remake your heart. His plan is nothing short of a total transformation: "He decided from the outset to shape the lives of those who love him along the same lines as the life of his Son" (Rom. 8:29 MSG).

"You have begun to live the new life, in which you are being made new and are becoming like the One who made you. This new life brings you the true knowledge of God" (Col. 3:10).

God is willing to change us into the likeness of the Savior. Shall we accept his offer? Here is my suggestion. Let's imagine what it means to be just like Jesus. Let's look long into the heart of Christ. Let's spend some chapters considering his compassion, reflecting upon his intimacy with the Father, admiring his focus, pondering his endurance. How did he forgive? When did he pray? What made him so pleasant? Why didn't he give up? Let's "fix our eyes on Jesus" (Heb. 12:2 NIV). Perhaps in seeing him, we will see what we can become.

Be gentle and ready to forgive;
never hold grudges. Remember, the Lord
forgave you, so you must forgive others.

COLOSSIANS 3:13 TLB

Chapter Two

Loving the People You Are Stuck With

A Forgiving Heart

MY FIRST PET CAME IN THE FORM OF A childhood Christmas Eve gift. Somewhere I have a snapshot of a brown-and-white Chinese pug, small enough to fit in my father's hand, cute enough to steal my eight-year-old heart. We named her Liz.

I carried her all day. Her floppy ears fascinated me, and her flat nose intrigued me. I even took her to bed. So what if she smelled like a dog? I thought the odor was cute. So what if she whined and whimpered? I thought the noise was cute. So what if she did her business on my pillow? Can't say I thought that was cute, but I didn't mind.

Mom and Dad had made it clear in our prenuptial agreement that I was to be Liz's caretaker, and I was happy to oblige. I cleaned her little eating dish and opened her can of puppy food. The minute she lapped up some water, I replenished it. I kept her hair combed and her tail wagging.

Within a few days, however, my feelings changed a bit. Liz was still my dog, and I was still her friend, but I grew weary with her barking, and she seemed hungry an awful lot. More than once my folks had to remind me, "Take care of her. She is your dog."

I didn't like hearing those words—*your dog*. I wouldn't have minded the phrase "your dog to play with" or "your dog when you want her" or even "your dog when she is behaving." But those weren't my parents' words. They said, "Liz is *your dog.*" Period. In sickness and in health. For richer, for poorer. In dryness and in wetness.

That's when it occurred to me. *I am stuck with Liz.*

The courtship was over, and the honeymoon had ended. We were mutually leashed. Liz went from an option to an obligation, from a pet to a chore, from someone to play with to someone to care for.

Perhaps you can relate. Chances are you know the claustrophobia that comes with commitment. Only instead of being reminded, "She is your dog," you're told, "He is your husband." Or, "She is your wife." Or, "He is your child, parent, employee or boss or room-mate" or any other relationship that requires loyalty for survival.

Some opt to flee: to get out of the relationship and start again elsewhere, though they are often surprised when the condition surfaces on the other side of the fence as well. Others fight. Houses become combat zones and offices become boxing rings, and tension becomes a way of life. A few, however, discover another treatment: forgiveness. My manual has no model for how forgiveness occurs, but the Bible does.

Jesus himself knew the feeling of being stuck with someone. For three years he ran with the same crew.

By and large, he saw the same dozen or so faces around the table, around the campfire, around the clock. They rode in the same boats and walked the same roads and visited the same houses, and I wonder, how did Jesus stay so devoted to his men? Not only did he have to put up with their visible oddities, he had to endure their invisible foibles. Think about it. He could hear their unspoken thoughts. He knew their private doubts. Not only that, he knew their future doubts. What if you knew every mistake your loved ones had ever made and every mistake they would ever make? What if you knew every thought they would have about you, every irritation, every dislike, every betrayal?

Was it hard for Jesus to love Peter, knowing Peter would someday curse him? Was it tough to trust Thomas, knowing Thomas would one day question Jesus' resurrection? How did Jesus resist the urge to recruit a new batch of followers? John wanted to destroy one enemy. Peter sliced off the ear of another. Just days before Jesus' death, his disciples were arguing about which of them was the best! How was he able to love people who were hard to like?

Few situations stir panic like being trapped in a relationship. For that reason I think it wise that we begin our study of what it means to have a heart like Jesus by pondering his heart of forgiveness. How was Jesus able to love his disciples? The answer is found in the thirteenth chapter of John.

With Towel and Basin

Of all the times we see the bowing knees of Jesus, none is so precious as when he kneels before his disciples and washes their feet.

It has been a long day. Jerusalem is packed with Passover guests, most of whom clamor for a glimpse of the Teacher. The spring sun is warm. The streets are dry. And the disciples are a long way from home. A splash of cool water would be refreshing.

The disciples enter, one by one, and take their places around the table. On the wall hangs a towel, and on the floor sits a pitcher and a basin. Any one of the disciples could volunteer for the job, but not one does.

After a few moments, Jesus stands and removes his outer garment. He wraps a servant's girdle around his waist, takes up the basin, and kneels before one of the disciples. He unlaces a sandal and gently lifts the foot and places it in the basin, covers it with water, and begins to bathe it. One by one, one grimy foot after another, Jesus works his way down the row.

In Jesus' day the washing of feet was a task reserved not just for servants but for the lowest of servants. Every circle has its pecking order, and the circle of household workers was no exception. The servant at the bottom of the totem pole was expected to be the one on his knees with the towel and basin.

You can be sure Jesus knows the future of these feet he is washing. These twenty-four feet will not spend the next day following their master, defending his cause. These feet will dash for cover at the flash of a Roman sword. Only one pair of feet won't abandon him in the garden. One disciple won't desert him at Gethsemane—Judas won't even make it that far! He will abandon Jesus that very night at the table.

I looked for a Bible translation that reads, "Jesus washed all the disciples' feet except the feet of Judas," but I couldn't find one. What a passionate moment when Jesus silently lifts the feet of his betrayer and washes them in the basin! Within hours the feet of Judas, cleansed by the kindness of the one he will betray, will stand in Caiaphas's court.

Behold the gift Jesus gives his followers! He knows what these men are about to do. He knows they are about to perform the vilest act of their lives. By morning they will bury their heads in shame and look down at their feet in disgust. And when they do, he wants them to remember how his knees knelt before them and he washed their feet. He wants them to realize those feet are still clean. "You don't understand now what I am doing, but you will understand later" (John 13:7).

Remarkable. He forgave their sin before they even

committed it. He offered mercy before they even sought it.

From the Basin of His Grace

Oh, I could never do that, you object. *The hurt is so deep. The wounds are so numerous. Just seeing the person causes me to cringe.* Perhaps that is your problem. Perhaps you are seeing the wrong person, or at least too much of the wrong person. Remember, the secret of having a heart like Jesus is "fixing our eyes" on him. Try shifting your glance away from the one who hurt you and setting your eyes on the one who has saved you.

"If I, your Lord and Teacher, have washed your feet, you also should wash each other's feet. I did this as an example so that you should do as I have done for you" (John 13:14–15).

Jesus washes our feet for two reasons. The first is to give us mercy; the second is to give us a message, and that message is simply this: Jesus offers unconditional grace; we are to offer unconditional grace. The mercy of Christ preceded our mistakes; our mercy must precede the mistakes of others. Those in the circle of Christ had no doubt of his love; those in our circles should have no doubts about ours.

What does it mean to have a heart like his? It means to kneel as Jesus knelt, touching the grimy parts of the people we are stuck with and washing away their unkindnesses with kindness. Or as Paul wrote, "Be kind and loving to each other, and forgive each other just as God forgave you in Christ" (Eph. 4:32).

"But, Max," you are saying, "I've done nothing wrong. I'm not the one who cheated. I'm not the one who lied. I'm not the guilty party here." Perhaps you aren't. But neither was Jesus. Of all the men in that room, only one was worthy of having his feet washed. And he was the one who washed the feet. The one worthy of being served, served others. The genius of Jesus' example is that the burden of bridge-building falls on the strong one, not on the weak one. The one who is innocent is the one who makes the gesture.

And you know what happens? More often than

not, if the one in the right volunteers to wash the feet of the one in the wrong, both parties get on their knees. Don't we all think we are right? Hence we wash each other's feet.

Please understand. *Relationships don't thrive because the guilty are punished but because the innocent are merciful.*

The Power of Forgiveness

Recently I shared a meal with some friends. A husband and wife wanted to tell me about a storm they were weathering. Through a series of events, she learned of an act of infidelity that had occurred over a decade ago. He had made the mistake of thinking it'd be better not to tell her, so he didn't. But she found out. And as you can imagine, she was deeply hurt.

Through the advice of a counselor, the couple dropped everything and went away for several days. A decision had to be made. Would they flee, fight, or forgive? So they prayed. They talked. They walked. They reflected. In this case the wife was clearly in the right. She could have left. Women have done so for lesser reasons. Or she could have stayed and made his life a living hell. Other women have done that. But she chose a different response.

On the tenth night of their trip, my friend found a card on his pillow. On the card was a printed verse: "I'd rather do nothing with you than something without you." Beneath the verse she had written these words:

I forgive you. I love you. Let's move on.

The card might as well have been a basin. And the pen might as well have been a pitcher of water, for out of it poured pure mercy, and with it she washed her husband's feet.

Certain conflicts can be resolved only with a basin of water. Are any relationships in your world thirsty for mercy? Are there any sitting around your table who need to be assured of your grace? Jesus made sure his disciples had no reason to doubt his love. Why don't you do the same?

Do not merely listen to the word,
and so deceive yourselves. Do what it says.
Anyone who listens to the word but does
not do what it says is like a man who looks
at his face in a mirror and, after looking
at himself, goes away and immediately
forgets what he looks like.

JAMES 1:22–24 NIV

Chapter Three

Hearing God's Music

A Listening Heart

"LET HE WHO HAS EARS TO HEAR, USE THEM." More than once Jesus said these words. Eight times in the Gospels and eight times in the book of Revelation we are reminded that it's not enough just to have ears—it's necessary to use them.[1]

In one of his parables Jesus compared our ears to soil.[2] He told about a farmer who scattered seed (symbolic of the Word) in four different types of ground (symbolic of our ears). Some of our ears are like a hard road—unreceptive to the seed. Others have ears like rocky soil—we hear the Word but don't allow it to take root. Still others have ears akin to a weed patch—too overgrown, too thorny, with too much competition for the seed to have a chance. And then there are some who have ears that hear: well-tilled, discriminate, and ready to hear God's voice.

Please note that in all four cases the seed is the same seed. The sower is the same sower. What's different is not the message or the messenger—it's the listener. And if the ratio in the story is significant, three-fourths of the world isn't listening to God's voice. Whether the cause be hard hearts, shallow lives, or anxious minds, 75 percent of us are missing the message.

It's not that we don't have ears; it's that we don't use them.

"Let he who has ears to hear, use them." How long has it been since you had your hearing checked? When God throws seed your way, what is the result? May I raise a question or two to test how well you hear God's voice?

How Long Has It Been Since You Let God Have You?

I mean really *have* you? How long since you gave him a portion of undiluted, uninterrupted time listening for his voice? Apparently Jesus did. He made a deliberate effort to spend time with God.

Spend much time reading about the listening life of Jesus and a distinct pattern emerges. He spent regular time with God, praying and listening. Mark says, "Very early in the morning, while it was still dark, Jesus got up, left the house and went off to a solitary place, where he prayed" (Mark 1:35 NIV). Luke tells us, "Jesus often withdrew to lonely places and prayed" (Luke 5:16 NIV).

Let me ask the obvious: If Jesus, the Son of God, the sinless Savior of humankind, thought it worthwhile to clear his calendar to pray, wouldn't we be wise to do the same?

Not only did he spend regular time with God in prayer, he spent regular time in God's Word. Of course we don't find Jesus pulling a leather-bound New Testament from his satchel and reading it. We do, however, see the stunning example of Jesus, in the throes of the wilderness temptation, using the Word of God to deal with Satan. Three times he is tempted, and each time he repels the attack with the phrase: "It is written in the Scriptures" (Luke 4:4, 8, 12), and then he quotes a verse. Jesus is so familiar with Scripture that he not only knows the verse, he knows how to use it.

And then there's the occasion when Jesus was asked to read in the synagogue. He is handed the book of Isaiah the prophet. He finds the passage, reads it, and declares, "While you heard these words just now, they were coming true!" (Luke 4:21). We are given the picture of a person who knows his way around in Scripture and can recognize its fulfillment. If Jesus thought it wise to grow familiar with the Bible, shouldn't we do the same?

If we are to be just like Jesus, we must have a regular time of talking to God and listening to his Word.

Surrogate Spirituality

Wait a minute. Don't you do that. I know exactly what some of you are doing. You are tuning me out. *Lucado is talking about daily devotionals, eh? This is a good time for me to take a mental walk over to the fridge and see what we have to eat.*

I understand your reluctance. Some of us have tried to have a daily quiet time and have not been successful. Others of us have a hard time concentrating. And all of us are busy. So rather than spend time with God, listening for his voice, we'll let others spend time with him and then benefit from their experience. Let them tell us what God is saying. After all, isn't that why we pay preachers? Isn't that why we read Christian books? *These folks are good at daily devotions. I'll just learn from them.*

If that is your approach, your spiritual experiences are secondhand and not firsthand. Listening to God is a firsthand experience. When he asks for your attention, God doesn't want you to send a substitute;

he wants you. He invites you to vacation in his splendor. He invites you to feel the touch of his hand. He invites you to feast at his table. He wants to spend time with you. And with a little training, your time with God can be the highlight of your day.

A friend of mine married an opera soprano. She loves concerts. Her college years were spent in the music department, and her earliest memories are of keyboards and choir risers. He, on the other hand, leans more toward Monday Night Football and country music. He also loves his wife, so on occasion he attends an opera. The two sit side by side in the same auditorium, listening to the same music, with two completely different responses. He sleeps and she weeps.

I believe the difference is more than taste. It's training. She has spent hours learning to appreciate the art of music. He has spent none. Her ears are Geiger-counter sensitive. He can't differentiate between *staccato* and *legato*. But he is trying. Last time we talked about the concerts, he told me he is managing to stay awake. He may never have the same ear as his wife, but with time he is learning to listen and appreciate the music.

Learning to Listen

I believe we can, too. Equipped with the right tools, we can learn to listen to God. What are those tools? Here are the ones I have found helpful.

A regular time and place. Select a slot on your schedule and a corner of your world, and claim it for God. For some it may be best to do this in the morning. "In the morning my prayer comes before you" (Ps. 88:13 NIV). Others prefer the evening and agree with David's prayer, "Let my . . . praise [be] like the evening sacrifice" (Ps. 141:2). Others prefer many encounters during the day. Apparently the author of Psalm 55 did. He wrote, "Evening, morning and noon I cry out" (v. 17 NIV).

Some sit under a tree, others in the kitchen. Maybe your commute to work or your lunch break would be appropriate. Find a time and place that seems right for you.

How much time should you take? As much as you need. Value quality over length. Your time with God should last long enough for you to say what you want and for God to say what he wants. Which leads us to a second tool you need—*an open Bible.*

God speaks to us through his Word. The first step in reading the Bible is to ask God to help you understand it. "But the Helper will teach you everything and will cause you to remember all that I told you. This Helper is the Holy Spirit whom the Father will send in my name" (John 14:26).

Before reading the Bible, pray. Don't go to Scripture looking for your own idea; go searching for God's. Read the Bible prayerfully. Also, read the Bible carefully. Jesus told us, "Search, and you will find" (Matt. 7:7). God commends those who "chew on Scripture day and night" (Ps. 1:2 MSG). The Bible is not a newspaper to be skimmed but rather a mine to be quarried. "Search for it like silver, and hunt for it like hidden treasure. Then you will understand respect for the LORD, and you will find that you know God" (Prov. 2:4–5).

Here is a practical point. Study the Bible a little at a time. God seems to send messages as he did his manna: one day's portion at a time. He provides "a command here, a command there. A rule here, a rule there. A little lesson here, a little lesson there" (Isa. 28:10). Choose depth over quantity. Read until a verse "hits" you, then stop and meditate on it. Copy the verse onto a sheet of paper, or write it in your journal, and reflect on it several times.

On the morning I wrote this, for example, my quiet time found me in Matthew 18. I was only four verses into the chapter when I read, *"The greatest person in the kingdom of heaven is the one who makes himself humble like this child."* I needed to go no further. I copied the words in my journal and pondered them on and off during the day. Several times I asked God, "How can I be more childlike?" By the end of the day, I was reminded of my tendency to hurry and my proclivity to worry.

Will I learn what God intends? If I listen, I will.

Don't be discouraged if your reading reaps a small

harvest. Some days a lesser portion is all we need. A little girl returned from her first day at school. Her mom asked, "Did you learn anything?" "I guess not," the girl responded. "I have to go back tomorrow and the next day and the next day . . ."

Such is the case with learning. And such is the case with Bible study. Understanding comes a little at a time, over a lifetime.

There is a third tool for having a productive time with God. Not only do we need a regular time and an open Bible, we also need *a listening heart*. Don't forget the admonition from James: "The man who looks into the perfect law, the law of liberty, and makes a habit of so doing, is not the man who hears and forgets. He puts that law into practice and he wins true happiness" (James 1:25 PHILLIPS).

We know we are listening to God when what we read in the Bible is what others see in our lives. Paul urged his readers to put into practice what they had learned from him. "What you have learned and received and heard and seen in me, do" (Phil. 4:9 RSV).

If you want to have a heart like Jesus, let God have you. Spend time listening for him until you receive your lesson for the day—then apply it.

A regular time and place.

An open Bible.

An open heart.

Our faces, then, are not covered.
We all show the Lord's glory, and we are
being changed to be like him. This change
in us brings ever greater glory, which
comes from the Lord, who is the Spirit.

2 CORINTHIANS 3:18

Sunlight poured from his face.

MATTHEW 17:2 MSG

Chapter Four

A Changed Face and a Set of Wings

A Worship-Hungry Heart

PEOPLE ON A PLANE AND PEOPLE ON A PEW have a lot in common. All are on a journey. Most are well-behaved and presentable. Some doze, and others gaze out the window. Most, if not all, are satisfied with a predictable experience. For many, the mark of a good flight and the mark of a good worship assembly are the same. "Nice," we like to say. "It was a nice flight / It was a nice worship service." We exit the same way we enter, and we're happy to return next time.

A few, however, are not content with nice. They

long for something more. The boy who just passed me did. I heard him before I saw him. I was already in my seat when he asked, "Will they really let me meet the pilot?" He was either lucky or shrewd because he made the request just as he entered the plane. The question floated into the cockpit, causing the pilot to lean out.

"Someone looking for me?" he asked.

The boy's hand shot up like he was answering his second-grade teacher's question. "I am!"

"Well, come on in."

With a nod from his mom, the youngster entered the cockpit's world of controls and gauges and emerged minutes later with eyes wide. "Wow!" he exclaimed. "I'm so glad to be on this plane!"

No one else's face showed such wonder. I should know. I paid attention. The boy's interest piqued mine, so I studied the faces of the other passengers but found no such enthusiasm. I mostly saw contentment: travelers content to be on the plane, content to be closer to their destination, content to be out of the airport, content to sit and stare and say little.

There were a few exceptions. The five or so mid-age women wearing straw hats and carrying beach-bags weren't content; they were exuberant. They giggled all the way down the aisle. My bet is they were moms-set-free-from-kitchens-and-kids. The fellow in the blue suit across the aisle wasn't content; he was cranky. He opened his laptop and scowled at its screen the entire trip. Most of us, however, were happier than he and more contained than the ladies. Most of us were content. Content with a predictable, uneventful flight. Content with a "nice" flight.

And since that is what we sought, that is what we got. The boy, on the other hand, wanted more. He wanted to see the pilot. If asked to describe the flight, he wouldn't say "nice." He'd likely produce the plastic wings the pilot gave him and say, "I saw the man up front."

Do you see why I say that people on a plane and people on a pew have a lot in common? Enter a church sanctuary and look at the faces. A few are giggly, a couple are cranky, but by and large we are content. Content to be there. Content to sit and look straight ahead and leave when the service is over. Content to enjoy an assembly with no surprises or turbulence. Content with a "nice" service. "Seek and you will find," Jesus promised.[1] And since a nice service is what we seek, a nice service is usually what we find.

A few, however, seek more. A few come with the childlike enthusiasm of the boy. And those few leave as he did, wide-eyed with the wonder of having stood in the presence of the pilot himself.

Come Asking

The same thing happened to Jesus. The day Jesus went to worship, his very face was changed.

You're telling me that Jesus went to worship?

I am. The Bible speaks of a day when Jesus took time to stand with friends in the presence of God. Let's read about the day Jesus went to worship:

> Six days later, Jesus took Peter, James, and John, the brother of James, up on a high mountain by themselves. While they watched, Jesus' appearance

was changed; his face became bright like the sun, and his clothes became white as light. Then Moses and Elijah appeared to them, talking with Jesus.

Peter said to Jesus, "Lord, it is good that we are here. If you want, I will put up three tents here— one for you, one for Moses, and one for Elijah."

While Peter was talking, a bright cloud covered them. A voice came from the cloud and said, "This is my Son, whom I love, and I am very pleased with him. Listen to him!" (Matt. 17:1–5)

The words of Matthew presuppose a decision on the part of Jesus to stand in the presence of God. The simple fact that he chose his companions and went up on a mountain suggests this was no spur-of-the-moment action. He didn't awaken one morning, look at the calendar and then at his watch, and say, "Oops, today is the day we go to the mountain." No, he had preparations to make. Ministry to people was suspended so ministry to his heart could occur. Since his chosen place of worship was some distance away, he had to select the right path and stay on the right road. By the time he was on the mountain, his heart was ready. Jesus prepared for worship.

Let me ask you, do you do the same? Do you prepare for worship? What paths do you take to lead you up the mountain? The question may seem foreign, but my hunch is, many of us simply wake up and show up. We're sadly casual when it comes to meeting God.

Would we be so lackadaisical with, oh, let's say, the president? Suppose you were granted a Sunday morning breakfast at the White House. How would you spend Saturday night? Would you get ready? Would you collect your thoughts? Would you think about your questions and requests? Of course you would. Should we prepare any less for an encounter with the Holy God?

Let me urge you to come to worship prepared to worship. Pray before you come so you will be ready to pray when you arrive. Sleep before you come so you'll stay alert when you arrive. Read the Word before you come so your heart will be soft when you worship. Come hungry. Come willing. Come expecting God to speak. Come asking, even as you walk through the door, "Can I see the pilot today?"

Reflecting His Glory

As you do, you'll discover the purpose of worship—to change the face of the worshiper. This is exactly what happened to Christ on the mountain. Jesus' appearance was changed: "His face became bright like the sun" (Matt. 17:2).

The connection between the face and worship is more than coincidental. Our face is the most public part of our bodies, covered less than any other area. It is also the most recognizable part of our bodies. We don't fill a school annual with photos of people's feet, but rather with photos of faces. God desires to take our faces, this exposed and memorable part of our bodies, and use them to reflect his goodness. Paul writes: "Our faces, then, are not covered. We all show the Lord's glory, and we are being changed to be like him. This change in us brings ever greater glory, which comes from the Lord, who is the Spirit" (2 Cor. 3:18).

God invites us to see his face so he can change ours. He uses our uncovered faces to display his glory. The transformation isn't easy. The sculptor of Mount Rushmore faced a lesser challenge than does God. But our Lord is up to the task. He loves to change the faces of his children. By his fingers, wrinkles of worry are rubbed away. Shadows of shame and doubt become portraits of grace and trust. He relaxes clenched jaws and smoothes furrowed brows. His touch can remove the bags of exhaustion from beneath the eyes and turn tears of despair into tears of peace.

How? Through worship.

We'd expect something more complicated, more demanding. A forty-day fast or the memorization of Leviticus perhaps. No. God's plan is simpler. He changes our faces through worship.

Exactly what is worship? I like King David's definition. "Oh magnify the LORD with me, and let us exalt His name together" (Ps. 34:3 NASB). Worship is the act of magnifying God. Enlarging our vision of him. Stepping into the cockpit to see where he sits and observe how he works. Of course, his size doesn't change, but our perception of him does. As we draw nearer, he seems larger. Isn't that what we need? A *big* view of God? Don't we have *big* problems, *big* worries, *big* questions? Of course we do. Hence we need a big view of God.

Worship offers that. How can we sing, "Holy, Holy, Holy" and not have our vision expanded? Or what about the lines from "It Is Well with My Soul"?

My sin—O the bliss of this glorious thought,
My sin—not in part but the whole,
Is nailed to the cross and I bear it no more,
Praise the Lord, praise the Lord, O my soul![1]

Can we sing those words and not have our countenance illuminated?

A vibrant, shining face is the mark of one who has stood in God's presence. After speaking to God, Moses had to cover his face with a veil (Exod. 34:33–35). After seeing heaven, Stephen's face glowed like that of an angel (Acts 6:15; 7:55–56).

God is in the business of changing the face of the world.

Let me be very clear. This change is his job, not ours. Our goal is not to make our faces radiant. Not even Jesus did that. Matthew says, "Jesus' appearance was changed," not "Jesus changed his appearance." Moses didn't even know his face was shining (Exod. 34:29). Our goal is not to conjure up some fake, frozen expression. Our goal is simply to stand before God with a prepared and willing heart and then let God do his work.

And he does. He wipes away the tears. He mops away the perspiration. He softens our furrowed brows. He touches our cheeks. He changes our faces as we worship.

Do you come to church with a worship-hungry heart? Our Savior did.

May I urge you to be just like Jesus? Prepare your heart for worship. Let God change your face through worship. Demonstrate the power of worship. Above all, seek the face of the pilot. The boy did. Because he sought the pilot, he left with a changed face and a set of wings. The same can happen to you.

Be self-controlled and alert.

Your enemy the devil prowls around like a

roaring lion looking for someone to devour.

Resist him, standing firm in the faith.

1 Peter 5:8–9 niv

Chapter Five

The Greenhouse
of the Mind

A Pure Heart

SUPPOSE YOU COME TO VISIT ME ONE DAY and find me working in my greenhouse. (Neither my house nor my thumb is green, but let's pretend.) I explain to you that the greenhouse was a gift from my father. He used state-of-the-art equipment to create the ideal structure for growth. The atmosphere is perfect. The lighting exact. The temperature is suited for flowers, fruit, or anything I want, and what I want is flowers and fruit.

I ask you to join me as I collect some seeds to

plant. You've always thought I was a bit crazy, but what I do next removes all doubt. You watch me walk into a field and strip seeds off of weeds. Crab grass seeds, dandelion seeds, grass burr seeds. I fill a bag with a variety of weed seeds and return to the greenhouse.

You can't believe what you've just seen. "I thought you wanted a greenhouse full of flowers and fruit."

"I do."

"Then don't you think you ought to plant flower seeds and fruit seeds?"

"Do you have any idea how much those seeds cost? Besides, you have to drive all the way to the garden center to get them. No thanks, I'm taking the cheap and easy route."

You walk away mumbling something about one brick short of a load.

The Greenhouse of the Heart

Everybody knows you harvest what you sow. You reap what you plant. Yet strangely, what we know when we develop land, we tend to forget when we cultivate our hearts.

Think for a moment of your heart as a greenhouse. The similarities come quickly. It, too, is a magnificent gift from your Father. It, too, is perfectly suited for growing. And your heart, like a greenhouse, has to be managed.

Consider for a moment your thoughts as seed. Some thoughts become flowers. Others become weeds. Sow seeds of hope and enjoy optimism. Sow seeds of doubt and expect insecurity. "People harvest only what they plant" (Gal. 6:7).

The proof is everywhere you look. Ever wonder why some people have the Teflon capacity to resist negativism and remain patient, optimistic, and forgiving? Could it be that they have diligently sown seeds of goodness and are enjoying the harvest?

Ever wonder why others have such a sour outlook? Such a gloomy attitude? You would, too, if your heart were a greenhouse of weeds and thorns.

If the heart is a greenhouse and our thoughts are

seeds, shouldn't we be careful about what we sow? Shouldn't we be selective about the seeds we allow to come into the greenhouse? Shouldn't there be a sentry at the door? Isn't guarding the heart a strategic task? According to the Bible it is: "Above all else, guard your heart, for it is the wellspring of life" (Prov. 4:23 NIV). Or as another translation reads: "Be careful what you think, because your thoughts run your life."

What a true statement! Test the principle, and see if you don't agree.

Two drivers are stuck in the same traffic jam. One person stews in anger, thinking, *My schedule is messed up.* The other sighs in relief, *Good chance to slow down.*

Two mothers face the same tragedy. One is destroyed: *I'll never get over this.* The other is despondent but determined: *God will get me through.*

Two executives face the same success. One pats himself on the back and grows cocky. The other gives the credit to God and grows grateful.

Two husbands commit the same failure. One bitterly assumes God's limit of grace has been crossed.

The other gratefully assumes a new depth of God's grace has been discovered.

"Above all else, guard your heart, for it is the wellspring of life."

For most of us, thought management is, well, unthought of. We think much about time management, weight management, personnel management, even scalp management. But what about thought management? Shouldn't we be as concerned about managing our thoughts as we are about managing anything else? Jesus was. Like a trained soldier at the gate of a city, he stood watch over his mind. He stubbornly guarded the gateway of his heart. Many thoughts were denied entrance. Need a few examples?

How about arrogance? On one occasion the people determined to make Jesus their king. What an attractive thought. Most of us would delight in the notion of royalty. Even if we refused the crown, we would enjoy considering the invitation. Not Jesus. "Jesus saw that in their enthusiasm, they were about to grab him and make him king, so he slipped off and went back up the mountain to be by himself" (John 6:15 MSG).

Another dramatic example occurred in a conversation Jesus had with Peter. Upon hearing Jesus announce his impending death on the cross, the impetuous apostle objected. "Impossible, Master! That can never be!" (Matt. 16:22 MSG). Apparently, Peter was about to question the necessity of Calvary. But he never had a chance. Christ blocked the doorway. He sent both the messenger and the author of the heresy scurrying: "Peter, get out of my way. Satan, get lost. You have no idea how God works" (Matt. 16:23 MSG).

And how about the time Jesus was mocked? Have you ever had people laugh at you? Jesus did, too. Responding to an appeal to heal a sick girl, he entered her house only to be told she was dead. His response? "The child is not dead but sleeping." The response of the people in the house? "They laughed at him." Just like all of us, Jesus had to face a moment of humiliation. But unlike most of us, he refused to receive it. Note his decisive response: "he put them all outside" (Mark 5:39–40 RSV). The mockery was not allowed in the house of the girl nor in the mind of Christ.

Jesus guarded his heart. If he did, shouldn't we do the same? Most certainly! "Be careful what you think, because your thoughts run your life" (Prov. 4:23). Jesus wants your heart to be fertile and fruitful. He wants you to have a heart like his. That is God's goal for you. He wants you to "think and act like Christ Jesus" (Phil. 2:5). But how? The answer is surprisingly simple. We can be transformed if we make one decision: *I will submit my thoughts to the authority of Jesus.*

To have a pure heart, we must submit all thoughts to the authority of Christ. If we are willing to do that, he will change us to be like him. Here is how it works.

A Guard at the Doorway

Let's return to the image of the greenhouse. Your heart is a fertile greenhouse ready to produce good fruit. Your mind is the doorway to your heart—the strategic place where you determine which seeds are sown and which seeds are discarded. The Holy Spirit is ready to help you manage and filter the thoughts that try to enter. He can help you guard your heart.

He stands with you on the threshold. A thought approaches, a questionable thought. Do you throw open the door and let it enter? Of course not. You "fight to capture every thought until it acknowledges the authority of Christ" (2 Cor. 10:5 PHILLIPS). You don't leave the door unguarded. You stand equipped with handcuffs and leg irons, ready to capture any thought not fit to enter.

For the sake of discussion, let's say a thought of temptation comes your way. If you're a fellow, the thought is dressed in flashy red. If you're a female, the thought is the hunk you've always wanted. There is the brush of the hand, the fragrance in the air, and the invitation. "Come on, it's all right. We're consenting adults."

What do you do? Well, if you aren't under the authority of Christ, you throw open the door. But if you have the mind of Christ, you step back and say, "Not so fast. You'll have to get permission from my big brother." So you take this steamy act before Jesus and ask, "Yes or no?"

Nowhere does he answer more clearly than in 1 Corinthians 6 and 7: "We must not pursue the kind of sex that avoids commitment and intimacy, leaving us more lonely than ever. . . . Is it a good thing to have sexual relations? Certainly—but only within a certain context. It's good for a man to have a wife, and for a woman to have a husband. Sexual drives are strong, but marriage is strong enough to contain them" (6:18; 7:1–2 MSG).

Now armed with the opinion of Christ and the sword of the Spirit, what do you do? Well, if the tempter is not your spouse, close the door. If the invitation is from your spouse, then HUBBA HUBBA HUBBA.

The point is this: Guard the doorway of your heart. Submit your thoughts to the authority of Christ. The more selective you are about seeds, the more delighted you will be with the crop.

Sing to the LORD a new song;

sing to the LORD, all the earth.

Sing to the Lord and praise his name;

every day tell how he saves us.

PSALM 96:1–2

Rejoice that your names

are written in heaven.

LUKE 10:20 NIV

Chapter Six

When Heaven Celebrates

A Rejoicing Heart

My family did something thoughtful for me last night. They had a party in my honor—a surprise birthday party. Early last week I told Denalyn not to plan anything except a nice, family evening at a restaurant. She listened only to the restaurant part. I was unaware that half a dozen families were going to join us.

In fact, I tried to talk her into staying at home. "Let's have the dinner on another night," I volunteered. Andrea had been sick, Jenna had homework, and I'd spent the afternoon watching football games and felt lazy. Not really in a mood to get up and clean up and go out. I thought I'd have no problem convincing the girls to postpone the dinner. Boy, was I surprised! They wouldn't think of it. Each of my objections was met with a united front and a unanimous defense. My family made it clear—we were going out to eat.

Not only that, we were leaving on time. I consented and set about getting ready. But to their dismay, I moved too slowly. We were a study in contrasts. My attitude was *why hurry?* My daughters' attitude was *hurry up!* I was ho-hum. They were gung-ho. I was content to stay. They were anxious to leave. To be honest, I was bewildered by their actions. They were being uncharacteristically prompt. Curiously enthused. Why the big deal? I mean, I enjoy a night out as much as the next guy, but Sara giggled all the way to the restaurant.

Only when we arrived did their actions make sense. One step inside the door and I understood their enthusiasm. SURPRISE! No wonder they were acting differently. They knew what I didn't. They had seen what I hadn't. They'd already seen the table and stacked the gifts and smelled the cake. Since they knew about the party, they did everything necessary to see that I didn't miss it.

Jesus does the same for us. He knows about THE PARTY. In one of the greatest chapters in the Bible, Luke 15, he tells three stories. Each story speaks of something lost and of something found. A lost sheep. A lost coin. And a lost son. And at the end of each one, Jesus describes a party, a celebration. The shepherd throws the party for the lost-now-found sheep. The housewife throws a party because of the lost-now-found coin. And the father throws a party in honor of his lost-now-found son.

Three parables, each with a party. Three stories, each with the appearance of the same word: *happy*. Regarding the shepherd who found the lost sheep, Jesus says: "And when he finds it, he *happily* puts it on his shoulders and goes home" (vv. 5–6, italics mine). When the housewife finds her lost coin, she announces, "Be *happy* with me because I have found the coin that I lost" (v. 9, italics mine). And the father of the prodigal son explains to the reluctant older brother, "We had to celebrate and be *happy* because your brother was dead, but now he is alive. He was lost, but now he is found" (v. 32, italics mine).

The point is clear. Jesus is happiest when the lost are found. For him, no moment compares to the moment of salvation. For my daughters, the rejoicing began when I got dressed and in the car and on the road to the party. The same occurs in heaven. Let one child consent to be dressed in righteousness and begin the journey home and heaven pours the punch, strings the streamers, and throws the confetti. "There is joy in the presence of the angels of God when one sinner changes his heart and life" (v. 10).

We don't always share such enthusiasm, do we? When you hear of a soul saved, do you drop everything and celebrate? Is your good day made better or your bad day salvaged? We may be pleased—but exuberant? Do our chests burst with joy? Do we feel an urge to call out the band and cut the cake and have a party? When a soul is saved, the heart of Jesus becomes the night sky on the Fourth of July, radiant with explosions of cheer.

Can the same be said about us? Perhaps this is one area where our hearts could use some attention.

God's Magnum Opus

Why do Jesus and his angels rejoice over one repenting sinner? Can they see something we can't? Do they know something we don't? Absolutely. They know what heaven holds. They've seen the table, and they've heard the music, and they can't wait to see your face when you arrive. Better still, they can't wait to see you.

When you arrive and enter the party, something wonderful will happen. A final transformation will occur. You will be just like Jesus. Drink deeply from 1 John 3:2: "We have not yet been shown what we will be in the future. But we know that when Christ comes again, *we will be like him*" (italics mine).

Of all the blessings of heaven, one of the greatest will be you! You will be God's magnum opus, his work of art. The angels will gasp. God's work will be completed. At last, you will have a heart like his.

You will love with a perfect love.

You will worship with a radiant face.

You'll hear each word God speaks.

Your heart will be pure, your words will be like jewels, your thoughts will be like treasures.

You will be just like Jesus. You will, at long last, have a heart like his. Envision the heart of Jesus and you'll be envisioning your own. Guiltless. Fearless. Thrilled and joyous. Tirelessly worshiping. Flawlessly discerning. As the mountain stream is pristine and endless, so will be your heart. *You will be like him.*

There is yet another reason for the celebration. Part of the excitement is from our arrival. The other part is from our deliverance. Jesus rejoices that we are headed to heaven, but he equally rejoices that we are saved from hell.

One phrase summarizes the horror of hell. "God isn't there."

According to Jesus, hell knows only one sound, the "weeping and gnashing of teeth" (Matt. 22:13 NIV). From hell comes a woeful, unending moan as its inhabitants realize the opportunity they have missed. What they would give for one more chance. But that chance is gone (Heb. 9:27).

To have a heart like his is to look into the faces of the saved and rejoice! They are just one grave away from being just like Jesus. To have a heart like his is to look into the faces of the lost and pray. For unless they turn, they are one grave away from torment.

And so my challenge to you is simple. Ask God to help you have his eternal view of the world. Every person you meet has been given an invitation to dinner. When one says yes, celebrate! And when one acts sluggish as I did last night, do what my daughters did. Stir him up and urge him to get ready. It's almost time for the party, and you don't want him to miss it.

Let us run the race that is
before us and never give up.

HEBREWS 12:1

Chapter Seven

Finishing Strong

An Enduring Heart

ON ONE OF MY SHELVES IS A BOOK ON "power abs." The cover shows a closeup of a fellow flexing his flat belly. His gut has more ripples and ridges than a pond on a windy day. Inspired, I bought the book, read the routine, and did the sit-ups . . . for a week.

Not far from the power-abs book is a tape series on speed reading. This purchase was Denalyn's idea, but when I read the ad, I was equally enthused. The course promises to do for my mind what *Power Abs* promised to do for my gut—turn it into steel. The back-cover copy promises that mastering this six-week series will enable you to read twice as fast and retain twice the amount. All you have to do is listen to the tapes—which I intend to do . . . someday.

And then there is my bottle of essential minerals. Thirty-two ounces of pure health. One swallow a day and I'll ingest my quota of calcium, chloride, magnesium, sodium, and sixty-six other vital earthly elements. (There's even a trace of iron, which is good since I missed my shot at the iron abs and the steel-trap mind.) The enthusiast who sold me the minerals convinced me that thirty dollars was a small price to pay for good health. I agree. I just keep forgetting to take them.

Don't get me wrong. Not everything in my life is incomplete. (This book is finished . . . well, almost.) But I confess, I don't always finish what I start. Chances are I'm not alone. Any unfinished projects under your roof? Perhaps an exercise machine whose primary function thus far has been to hold towels? Or an unopened do-it-yourself pottery course? How about a half-finished patio deck or a half-dug pool or a half-planted garden? And let's not even touch the topic of diets and weight loss, ok?

Actually, my desire is not to convince you to finish everything. My desire is to encourage you to finish the *right* thing. Certain races are optional—like washboard abs and speed reading. Other races are essential —like the race of faith. Consider this admonition from the author of Hebrews: "Let us run the race that is before us and never give up" (Heb. 12:1).

The Race

Had golf existed in the New Testament era, I'm sure the writers would have spoken of mulligans and foot wedges, but it didn't, so they wrote about running. The word *race* is from the Greek *agon,* from which we get the word *agony.* The Christian's race is not a jog but rather a demanding and grueling, sometimes agonizing race. It takes a massive effort to finish strong.

Likely you've noticed that many don't? Surely you've observed there are many on the side of the trail? They used to be running. There was a time when they kept the pace. But then weariness set in. They didn't think the run would be this tough. Or they were discouraged by a bump and daunted by a fellow runner. Whatever the reason, they don't run anymore. They may be Christians. They may come to church. They may put a buck in the plate and warm a pew, but their hearts aren't in the race. They retired before their time. Unless something changes, their best work will have been their first work, and they will finish with a whimper.

By contrast, Jesus' best work was his final work, and his strongest step was his last step. Our Master is the classic example of one who endured. The writer of Hebrews goes on to say that Jesus "held on while wicked people were doing evil things to him" (v. 3). The Bible says Jesus "held on," implying that Jesus could have "let go." The runner could have given up, sat down, gone home. He could have quit the race. But he didn't. "He held on while wicked people were doing evil things to him."

His own family called him a lunatic. His neighbors treated him even worse. When Jesus returned to his hometown, they tried to throw him off a cliff (Luke 4:29). But Jesus didn't quit running.

Such words stir one urgent question: How? Like Jesus we are tempted. Like Jesus we are accused. Like Jesus we are ashamed. But unlike Jesus, we give up. We give out. We sit down. How can we keep running as Jesus did? How can our hearts have the endurance Jesus had?

By focusing where Jesus focused—on "the joy that God put before him" (Heb. 12:2).

The Reward

This verse may very well be the greatest testimony ever written about the glory of heaven. Nothing is said about golden streets or angels' wings. No reference is made to music or feasts. Even the word *heaven* is missing from the verse. But though the word is missing, the power is not.

Remember, heaven was not foreign to Jesus. He is the only person to live on earth *after* he had lived in heaven. As believers, you and I will live in heaven after time on earth, but Jesus did just the opposite. He knew heaven before he came to earth. He knew what awaited him upon his return. And knowing what awaited him in heaven enabled him to bear the shame on earth.

He "accepted the shame as if it were nothing because of the joy that God put before him" (Heb. 12:2). In his final moments, Jesus focused on the joy God put before him. He focused on the prize of heaven. By focusing on the prize, he was able not only to finish the race but to finish it strong.

Jesus lifted his eyes beyond the horizon and saw the table. He focused on the feast. And what he saw gave him strength to finish—and finish strong.

Such a moment awaits us. In a world oblivious to power abs and speed reading, we'll take our place at the table. In an hour that has no end, we will rest. Surrounded by saints and engulfed by Jesus himself, the work will, indeed, be finished. The final harvest will have been gathered, we will be seated, and Christ will christen the meal with these words: "Well done, good and faithful servant" (Matt. 25:23 KJV).

And in that moment, the race will have been worth it.

May he enlighten the eyes of your mind

so that you can see what hope his call

holds for you, what rich glories he has

promised the saints will inherit.

EPHESIANS 1:18 NIV

Conclusion

THROUGHOUT THE PAGES OF THIS BOOK, we've been looking at what it means to have a heart like Jesus. The world has never known a heart so pure, a character so flawless. His spiritual hearing was so keen he never missed a heavenly whisper. His mercy so abundant he never missed a chance to forgive. No lie left his lips, no distraction marred his vision. He touched when others recoiled. He endured when others quit. Jesus is the ultimate model for every person. And what we have done in these pages is precisely what God invites you to do with the rest of your life. He urges you to fix your eyes upon Jesus. Heaven invites you to set the lens of your heart on the heart of the Savior and make him the object of your life.

Can you think of a greater gift than to be like Jesus? Christ felt no guilt; God wants to banish yours. Jesus had no bad habits; God wants to remove yours. Jesus had no fear of death; God wants you to be fearless. Jesus had kindness for the diseased and mercy for the rebellious and courage for the challenges. God wants you to have the same.

He loves you just the way you are, but

he refuses to leave you that way.

He wants you to be just like Jesus.

Notes

Chapter 1: A Heart Like Jesus
1. Adapted from Max Lucado, *A Gentle Thunder* (Dallas: Word Publishing, 1995), 46.
2. David Jeremiah audiotape: *The God of the Impossible*, TPR02.

Chapter 3: Hearing God's Music
1. Matt. 11:15, 13:9, 13:43; Mark 4:9, 4:23, 8:18; Luke 8:8, 14:35; Rev. 2:7, 2:11, 2:17, 2:29, 3:6, 3:13, 3:22, 13:9.
2. Mark 4:1–20.

Chapter 4: A Changed Face and a Set of Wings
1. Horatio G. Spafford, "It Is Well with My Soul."

Share the "Just Like Jesus" Message with Every Age

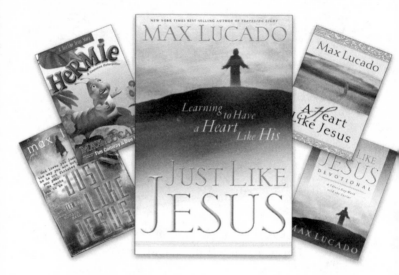

From Max Lucado
America's Leading Inspirational Author

FOR CHILDREN

Hermie: A Common Caterpillar
(VHS / DVD)

Hermie: A Common Caterpillar
(board book)

Hermie: A Common Caterpillar
(picture book)

(Hermie products also available in Spanish)

FOR TWEENS

Just Like Jesus

FOR YOU

Just Like Jesus (hardcover book)
(Also available in Spanish)
Just Like Jesus Devotional
A Heart Like Jesus